nature cards

nature cards

Making Greeting Cards, Invitations and Stationery

SUSAN JAWORSKI-STRANC

APPLE

Published in the UK in 2003 by
Apple Press
Sheridan House
112-116A Western Road
Hove
East Sussex BN3 1DD

ISBN: 1-84092-430-6

10 9 8 7 6 5 4 3 2 1

Cover Design: Nina Barnett
Cover Image: Bobbie Bush Photography, www.bobbiebush.com
Photography: Bobbie Bush Photography, www.bobbiebush.com,
     except for images on page 10 by Kevin Thomas
Templates and Illustrations: Lorraine Dey Studios
Project Manager and Copyeditor: Lindsay Stoms
Proofreader: Krista Fuller

Printed in Singapore

This book is dedicated
To my Mom, Janet,
Who has given me
Everlasting RAINBOWS
From a box of Crayolas
&
A packet of seeds.

Contents

Introduction

Welcome. A garden is a very special place. It offers an environment where the pressures of modern living can give way to joyous color and natural rhythms. How easy and pleasurable it is to reflect on life's larger relationships and complexities unfolding before your senses on a miniature scale in the garden. Anyone who loves to garden knows it as an endless source of creative and inspirational thought. Creating greeting cards that reflect your love and respect for this special haven is one way to share your personal message of hope, love, and understanding of the natural world.

In *Garden Greetings,* you'll find numerous projects, which are the poetic equivalents of life's many celebrations. Wonder at the animation of an unfolding flower as it reveals a special thought. The fluttering form of a butterfly is here to enjoy over and over again. Other card projects encourage you to share your garden's bounty. For example, there are card designs for sending harvested seeds, a favorite recipe, and even the ingredients for a humble cup of herbal tea. Use the metaphor of a simple trellis to reward upward growth, or the ceremonial swing of a garden gate as the opening to a new view of the world. Make stationery, send photos, and celebrate life's special occasions. Share your happiness with others and show them just how special and meaningful the garden is to you by making a garden greeting.

Projects found in this book are easily adapted for many special occasions, thoughts, and wishes. Each project can be viewed as a source of inspiration— a starting point for your own personal expression—or work that can be created exactly as described. These projects are easily adapted for persons of all abilities and levels of skill. It is my hope that you enjoy making and giving these beautiful cards, stationery, and invitations, and that they will create a lasting impression on your loved ones.

– Susan Jaworski-Stranc

Chapter 1

Getting Started

The start of any new art and craft activities is always an exciting adventure. Like an explorer embarking on an expedition, here in *Garden Greetings* there's enchanting terrain to follow, engaging techniques to learn, and enduring treasures to send off to family and friends.

The following list is offered as an aid to securing the necessary tools and materials you'll need to create the projects in *Garden Greetings*. Background information regarding different card formats and folding techniques concludes this chapter.

Always be on the lookout for interesting papers. Build an exotic paper collection to have on hand for future card-making projects of your own.

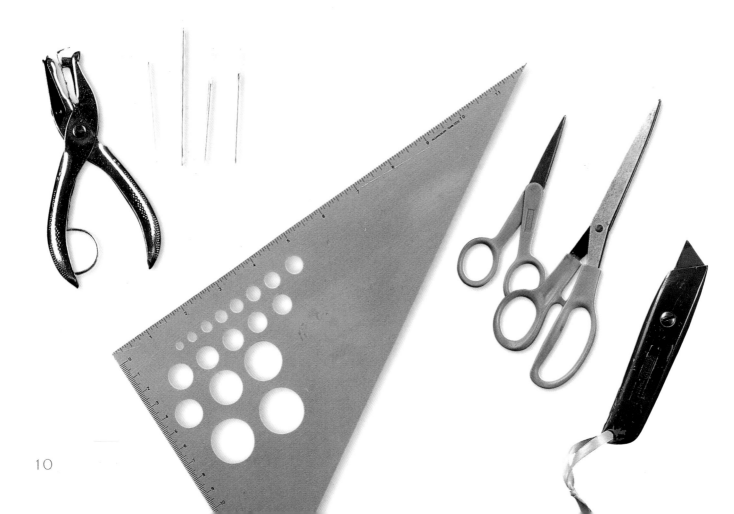

Toolbox

A **bodkin** is used in sewing, but is an excellent tool for piercing paper with small uniform holes. A sewing needle is a good substitute.

A **bone folder** (above right) is used for scoring lines on paper. This creasing or indenting of paper makes the process of paper folding easier. After folding paper along the crease, use the bone folder to make crisp, clean folds with a single swipe across the fold.

A **compass** is a necessary instrument for making circles. Also, they can be used as a type of ruler, dividing a line into equal segments.

A **craft knife** is an essential tool. Be sure to buy extra blades. Sharp blades will make cutting tasks safer and easier. Change the blades often.

A **mat knife** (opposite, fifth from left) or utility knife with break-away blades is used to cut heavy boards such as chipboard or mat board. Keep hands and fingers out of the line of cutting. Instead of trying to cut the mat board with one pass of the knife, use a series of gentle pressured cuts, going a

deeper each time, until the mat board is cut into two pieces.

A **punch** (opposite far left) is a tool that cuts small diameter holes in paper. There are two kinds of paper punches. One type makes holes by squeezing down on spring release handles. The other type is constructed with a sharp, circular blade, which is screwed into a solid metal cylinder and is struck with a hammer to make a hole. A big advantage to working with the second tool is that it can be placed anywhere on the paper surface.

Rulers (opposite, third from left) are an important measuring devise. Trans- parent rulers, used by quilters, are ideal for drawing parallel lines. Purchase a 12" to 18" (30 cm to 46 cm) metal ruler. It will last forever because of its strength and durability.

Scissors (opposite, forth from left), that are small and have fine points are essential for cutting delicate corners and edges.

A **self-healing mat board** will protect your tabletops and define your working area.

Adhesives

A term used for the grouping of glues, paste, and tapes. There are two types of adhesives available: dry and wet. Dry adhesives, such as glue sticks and double-sided tapes, have some superior qualities over wet adhesives, such as white glue. The paper will not buckle when the glue is applied and will not shrink when the glue is drying. Buy ¼" (6 mm)-wide rolls and 8" x 10" (20 cm x 25 cm) sheets of double-sided tape. One word of caution: these tapes are not removable and will damage the paper if an attempt is made to change paper positions. If you like working with wet adhesives, use a quick-drying type specially made for papers.

Fasteners

Eyelets and grommets offer a creative method of anchoring multiple papers together while adding a decorative element to card design. Use eyelets to enhance and strengthen punched holes.

A **paper brad** is a decorative item to facilitate movement such as the fanning out of papers while anchoring the papers together at one point source.

Plant Material

Fresh plant stems, such as herbs, can be used right from the garden without any special preparation in projects. Over time, they'll dry in the card arrangement. Use craft glue such as a water-based craft lacquer for adhering the stems to paper.

Pressing flowers and leaves can be done by carefully positioning them between the pages of a telephone book. Weight down the closed book with other heavy books. The drying process will take two weeks—a little longer if the humidity is high. Collect your flowers and leaves in the early morning and throughout the growing season, creating a fine collection of dried plant material for year-round card crafting. Also check out the dried flowers in florist shops or craft stores. Commercially made flower presses are available in craft stores as well.

Dry flower petals and herbs in a slow oven (225° F[107°C]) with the door slightly open or placed in a food dehydrator. Carefully monitor the drying progress to ensure proper treatment.

Harvested seeds and petals that have been air-dried should be saved in envelopes, plastic bags, or baby food jars to seal them from moisture. Used as embellishments similar to the use of beads in craft projects, seeds lend an earthy look and feel to your projects.

Translucent papers, such as vellum, have beautiful layering effects because of their atmospheric quality. Available at many fine art and craft stores, these papers come in many different colors and decorative patterns. A wide variety of oriental papers have translucent qualities as well, with inclusions of opaque fibers dispersed throughout the sheets.

Decorative papers, such as commercially printed papers, gift-wrapping paper, marbled paper, and a wide variety of origami papers should be part of your paper portfolio.

Card stock is a medium weight paper. It comes in a wide selection of colors and is the ideal base for card making. Watercolor art paper is also an excellent medium weight paper.

Chip board or heavy card stock is used for added strength and mounting. Shoeboxes are an excellent source for this type of material.

Folding

Often greeting cards are folded one of two ways. The first is called the half-fold where the paper is folded in half either along the long or short length. The second is called the quarter-fold where the paper is folded in half one more time and then opened and cut in two along the second fold.

To make the opening of the greeting card more intriguing for the recipient, there are several card formats worth trying.

French doors is a format in which the sides of the paper are folded to the center of the paper and open like French doors, hence the name. Projects that use this "French Door" style include the Decorated Photo Corner Frame (page 40), the "We've Moved" Birdhouse (page 82), and the Little Sprout Birth Announcement (page 84).

Dos à Dos is a format in which two folded cards are attached back to back to achieve a "Z" or zigzag format, or a single sheet of paper is divided into thirds and folded into a "Z" format. For a slight change in the "Z" format, reverse the direction of one section so both sections fold in toward the center. To prevent buckling of the inside section, trim a little off its edge so the card will close properly. Projects that use the "Dos à Dos" style include the Garden Silhouettes (page 49) and the Floral Monogram Tab Cards (page 28).

Origami is a popular Japanese art form of paper folding, usually without the aid of cutting or gluing. The Flutterbug Origami Greeting (page 53) features this style of folding.

A Word About Mailing

So, the card is absolutely beautiful and you're off to your local post office to mail the creation. Ask the postmaster for a handout explaining the postal regulations and the letter size standards template. If you have not planned your card design around the minimum size, proper height to length ratio, and thickness regulations, then a surcharge will be added to the regular postage.

If you are planning a mass mailing, be sure to stay within the postal regulations to save money. Otherwise, do not limit your creativity to save a few cents.

Have all your handcrafted cards hand-cancelled. If the card needs extra protection from possible crushing, then use envelopes with bubble pack inserts.

Making a handcrafted envelope is easy. Just place the card on a square piece of paper that has a length 1¼" (3.2 cm) longer than the card's largest dimension. Place the card on the square, creating four triangles along its perimeter. Fold the triangles over the card and seal with a sticker.

Chapter 2

Greeting Cards and Stationery: Seasons Handmade

Each season, distinct and unique, offers a plenitude of garden gifts.

Share your garden's abundance and experience the pleasure of enriching other people's lives. The simple act of creating one of these cards holds the promise of touching another's heart by sharing the connections you feel to the garden's earthly riches. Pass along a sense of well-being, wholesome thoughts, and feelings through the creation of handsome cards and stationery that weave the beauty of soft textures, herbal scents, and floral colors.

- *Compose a letter with the beauty of Japanese leaves layered beneath your writing.*

- *Gather a few sprigs of lavender that, upon the card's opening, release a delightful fragrance.*

- *Share a favorite garden recipe.*

- *Give the gift of relaxation with homemade tea.*

Dear Anne,

What a treat to visit with you in your beautiful garden.

The roses were so fragrant and th delphiniums so sky blue.

To sip tea among such beau birds hum, sing and r always delight in doing

Let us always fir strength to conti and godly work divinely grow t

Your T
Mar

Garden Motif Stationery

Design personal stationery as unique as your garden. Easily made with the stamping of large, simple garden forms onto paper, the design's soft boldness is sure to dance with delight under your printed words.

INSTRUCTIONS

1. Tear the paper into four 6" x 9" (15 cm x 23 cm) sheets using the ruler as a tearing edge.

2. Gently press the sponge stamp onto the selected stamping pad. Place the stamp into position on the surface of the stationery. Cover the stamp with a piece of scrap paper and press down with the palm of your hand. Remove the scrap paper and stamp.

3. Repeat stamping process until a satisfactory design is complete.

MATERIALS

- 12" x 18" (30 cm x 46 cm) best quality paper
- scrap paper
- sponge stamps—garden motifs, such as birds, trowel, watering can
- stamp pads—red, yellow, blue, and green
- ruler

HELPFUL HINT

If a stronger edge is desired after printing, use a colored pencil to redraw the outline of the stamped motif.

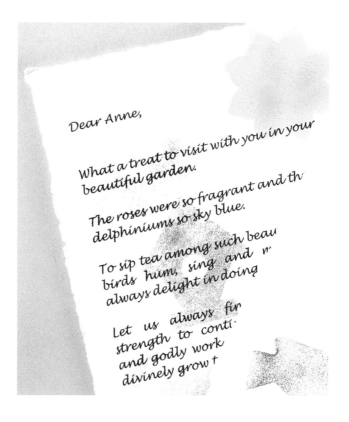

Dear Anne,

What a treat to visit with you in your beautiful garden.

The roses were so fragrant and th delphiniums so sky blue.

To sip tea among such beau birds hum, sing and n always delight in doing

Let us always fir strength to conti and godly work divinely grow †

Pressed Leaves Stationery

Leaf types come in a wide variety of forms. Many are quite beautiful to behold, such as the Red Japanese Maple. Their elegant shape makes an attractive "falling leaf" background to letter writing. Lift the translucent notepaper to have a closer look at each leaf's rich intricacies of vein and toothed edge.

INSTRUCTIONS

1. Arrange five or six leaves on the stationery into a pleasing composition.

2. Brush small amounts of white glue onto the back of a leaf, including the stem. Reposition the leaf on the stationery. Repeat with the remaining leaves.

3. Place a sheet of waxed paper over the stationery. Then place a heavy book over the project and leave it in position overnight.

4. Remove the waxed paper and the book.

5. Place a strip of double-sided tape across the top of the stationery. Remove the backing from the tape. Position the translucent paper over the stationery and adhere it into position.

MATERIALS

- 5½" x 8½" (14 cm x 21.6 cm) bright white stationery with matching envelope
- 5½" x 8½" (14 cm x 21.6 cm) translucent paper
- five or six assorted pressed maple leaves
- roll of ¼" (6 mm)-wide double-sided tape
- white glue
- #1 brush
- 5½" x 8½" (14 cm x 21.6 cm) waxed paper
- heavy book

Dried Flower Medallions

MATERIALS

- pressed flowers
- assortment of 2" (5 cm) squares of colored and translucent paper
- flower template (page 92)
- white glue
- craft knife
- scissors with a decorative edge, such as scalloped

HELPFUL HINT

Place the finished medallions back into the flower press for safekeeping.

Accentuate your pressed flowers with these colorful paper medallions. Fashion a colorful collection to use year round as "dash of summer" embellishments for your letters. Freely combine different sorts of papers to generate whimsical blooms.

INSTRUCTIONS

1. Stack papers in the following order: flower template, translucent paper, and colored paper.

2. Use a craft knife to cut along the inside edges of the flower petals. Next, use the decorative-edged scissors to cut out the flower.

3. Remove the template design. Rotate the translucent paper design until its petals are over the spaces between the colored paper petals.

4. Place a drop of glue in between the paper layers and in the center of the top paper.

5. Press a dried flower into the drop of glue.

Garden Recipe Cards

These recipe cards feature dancing chili peppers, a forest of asparagus, and intertwined carrots—a delightful feast for the eyes. Each card is decorated on one side with stamps and the other with a recipe. They slide in and out of windowed envelopes that are made using folded paper. The cards make thoughtful and inexpensive presents, especially when printed with friends' and family members' favorite recipes.

INSTRUCTIONS

1. Fold the colored paper in half. Using a bone folder, score a line $\frac{1}{2}$" (1.3 cm) from each of the open edges opposite the fold. Open the paper. Trim the $\frac{1}{2}$" (1.3 cm) strip from the right edge. Run a strip of double-sided tape along the left edge. Fold the paper in half. Fold over the $\frac{1}{2}$" (1.3 cm) strip to the back. Do not remove tape backing.

2. Transfer or trace the Mason jar shape onto the front of the paper. Open the paper and cut out the inside of the Mason jar. Don't cut directly on the outline of the jar, but rather make the cut $\frac{1}{8}$" (3 mm) inside the line.

3. Cut out a half circle, 1" (2.5 cm) wide, at the top and center of the paper, above the Mason jar. This will be the pull slot.

4. Fold the paper in half again. Fold over the $\frac{1}{2}$" (1.3 cm) strip to the back of the sleeve. Remove the tape backing and adhere the edges together.

5. Practice the basic printing techniques of the veggie foam rubber stamps on a piece of scrap paper. When you are confident with the techniques, begin printing on the white card stock. When the print is dry, enhance it using colored pencils.

MATERIALS

- 6" x 10" (15.2 cm x 25.4 cm) colored paper
- 3$\frac{3}{4}$" x 6" (9.5 cm x 15.2 cm) white card stock
- 12" (30 cm) length of $\frac{1}{4}$" (6 mm)-wide ribbon
- 1" (2.5 cm) circle sticker
- 4$\frac{1}{2}$" (11 cm) Mason jar template (page 92) or similar rubber stamp
- black marker or ink pad
- press set of veggie stamps
- craft knife
- paper punch
- roll of $\frac{1}{4}$" (6 mm)-wide double-sided tape
- acrylic paint set
- colored pencils
- watercolor brushes
- water cup
- bone folder
- ruler
- scrap paper

HELPFUL HINT

Other printing techniques can be just as effective as printing with foam rubber veggie shapes. Stencils or rubber stamps are great alternatives.

BROILED TOMATOES

Broil tomato halves, cut side up, 3 inches
from heat about 5 minutes until hot through.
If desired, blot with butter, season, and
sprinkle with crushed herbs before broiling.
OR, combine 1/2 cup dairy cream, 1/4 cup
mayonnaise, 2 tablespoons finely chopped
onions, 1/4 teaspoon dried dillweed, and 1/4
teaspoon salt. Spoon over hot broiled
tomatoes.

BAKED TOMATOES

Place tomato halves in shallow baking pan.
Sprinkle with seasoned salt and buttered
crumbs if desires. Baked at 375 about 20
minutes

6. Turn the card over and write or type the recipe
   on the back of the card.

7. Adhere one half of the circle sticker to the top
   and center of the printed side. Fold the rest of
   the sticker to the back. Punch a hole through
   the sticker. Fold the ribbon in half. Slip the fold
   through the hole from the back of the card. Pull
   the ribbon ends through the loop and pull tight.

8. Slip the recipe card into the Mason jar sleeve.

LAVENDER
Lavadula Angustifolia

Lavender and Vase

MATERIALS

- four to six stems of fresh lavender
- $5\frac{1}{2}$" x $8\frac{1}{2}$" (14 cm x 21.6 cm) heavy weight, metallic rose paper
- $5\frac{1}{2}$" x $8\frac{1}{2}$" (14 cm x 21.6 cm) decorative paper
- $5\frac{1}{2}$" x $8\frac{1}{2}$" (14 cm x 21.6 cm) mat board
- $5\frac{1}{2}$" x $8\frac{1}{2}$" (14 cm x 21.6 cm) sheet of double-sided tape
- 1" x 5" (2.5 cm x 12.7 cm) label
- ten $\frac{1}{2}$" (1.3 cm) foam sticky squares
- large rubber stamp of a vine background
- claret embossing powder
- water-based craft lacquer
- $2\frac{1}{2}$" (6.4 cm)-high rubber stamp vase
- black and maroon ink pads
- craft knife
- compass
- heat gun
- ruler

Dried lavender keeps its aromatic qualities for a long time. Create a simple floral arrangement using freshly cut or dried lavender stems and a stamped vase design. Any small leaf herb, such as thyme, can be used as well.

INSTRUCTIONS

1. Stamp the metallic paper with an overall design using the large stamp block. Sprinkle with claret colored embossing powder and adhere with heat gun.

2. Using a compass, draw a $2\frac{1}{2}$" (6.4 cm) circle on the back of the metallic paper, 1" (2.5 cm) from the top. Next, draw a $3\frac{1}{2}$" x 5" (8.9 cm x 12.7 cm) rectangle, 2" (5 cm) from the top. Using a craft knife, cut along the drawn lines, creating a frame.

3. Adhere ten sticky squares to the back—one in each corner and the remainder placed equally around the perimeter. Write the name of the herb on the label and adhere it to the front.

4. Adhere the sheet of double-sided tape to the mat board. Remove the backing and place the decorative paper on top.

5. Remove the backing paper from the sticky squares on the metallic paper and place the metallic frame onto the decorative paper. Stamp the vase and arrange plant stems within the vase.

6. Fill the inside area of the vase with a thin layer of craft lacquer, tacking down the stems. Let dry. Repeat this step until the vase looks three-dimensional.

Floral Monogram Tab Cards

With the use of subtle colors and a large floral block letter, this elegant card spells "sophistication." The design could easily be adapted as an invitation for a special event, or fashion a set of five and give them as a gift to a newly wedded couple.

INSTRUCTIONS

1. Turn the floral paper face down. Adhere the contrasting floral paper to one half of the larger paper using the sheet of double-sided tape. Fold the large sheet of paper in half with the contrasting paper on top and facing up.

2. With the fold to your left, draw a vertical line dividing this section in two. Next, center the square template on the drawn line. Trace the sides of the square to the right of the dividing line.

3. Unfold the paper. Using a craft knife, cut the traced lines. Fold along the drawn line, creating a square. Unfold and place a strip of double-sided tape along the $5\frac{1}{2}$" (14 cm) edge. Fold over again and adhere.

4. Stamp a letter in the newly created square.

MATERIALS

- $5\frac{1}{2}$" x $8\frac{1}{2}$" (14 cm x 21.6 cm) floral paper
- $5\frac{1}{2}$" x $4\frac{1}{4}$" (14 cm x 10.8 cm) contrasting floral paper
- roll of $\frac{1}{4}$" (6 mm)-wide double-sided tape
- $5\frac{1}{2}$" x $4\frac{1}{4}$" (14 cm x 10.8 cm) sheet of double-sided tape
- 2" (5.1 cm) square template cut from card stock
- craft knife
- floral alphabet block letters
- ink pad
- ruler

HELPFUL HINT

Nervous about stamping on your newly created card? Experiment by stamping letters on extra floral paper. Trim away the chosen block letter and adhere to the card using double-sided tape or glue.

 GOING ONE STEP FURTHER

Insert a $5\frac{1}{2}$" x $4\frac{1}{4}$" (14 cm x 10.8 cm) note paper folded in half and adhere with a strip of double-sided tape to the inside of the folded card. Also, $\frac{1}{4}$" (6 mm)-wide paper bands can give the card an added decorative element as well as a means of keeping the card closed.

*S*haring Seeds Greeting

If you are a seed saver, here's a creative way to package seeds and share them with your friends. The textural qualities of the packaged seeds are highlighted through the cut out stenciled letters. Although the illustrated design uses the aid of a computer to create an overall design, any decorative or brightly colored paper can be used just as effectively.

MATERIALS

- 8½" x 11" (21.6 cm x 27.9 cm) colored paper
- 2½" x 6¼" (6.4 cm x 15.9 cm) clear acetate
- roll of ¼" (6 mm)-wide double-sided tape
- 8½" x 11" (21.6 cm x 27.9 cm) colored paper
- 1⅛" (2.9 cm-high) letter stencils
- seeds
- craft knife
- pencil
- bone folder
- ruler
- folding diagrams (page 93)

INSTRUCTIONS

1. To fold a spine in the colored paper, position the sheet on a flat surface with the 8½" (21.6 cm) sides at the top and bottom. Fold the top edge down, leaving ¼" (6 mm) of the bottom edge of paper extending beyond the top edge, and then crease the fold. Turn the paper over, keeping the fold along the top. Lift the top edge and reposition it ¼" (6 mm) above the bottom edge, and crease it to make a second fold. These two folds should be ¼" (6 mm) apart, creating a spine in the center of the paper.

2. Decide the general area in which the stenciled letters will be placed. To create a guide for letter placement, use a pencil and draw a straight line.

3. Place the letter stencils along the pencil line. Trace the letters onto the paper. Use a craft knife to cut out the individual letters.

4. Refer to the five enlarged folding diagrams on page 93 (also on facing page) to assist with this step. On all four sides of the acetate, score a line ¼" (6 mm) from the edge. Score another set of four lines, ¼" (6 mm) in from the first set. Cut away a ½" x ½" (1.3 cm x 1.3 cm) square from each corner. To create the box shape, fold the inside scored sections in toward the center of the acetate. Next, fold the outside scored sections out away from the box. For each side, gently pull the edges upward making a right angle section. Place a strip of doublesided tape along the outer folded lip of each of the four sides of acetate that will come in contact with the card. Turn the box over.

5. Position the box under the cut out letters of colored paper. With a pencil, mark the corners onto the colored paper. Remove the backing from along one edge. Place into proper position on the back of the card and adhere. Repeat with the other two sides, leaving one short edge open.

6. Fill the box with seeds through the open side. Remove the backing from the tape and adhere the remaining side closed.

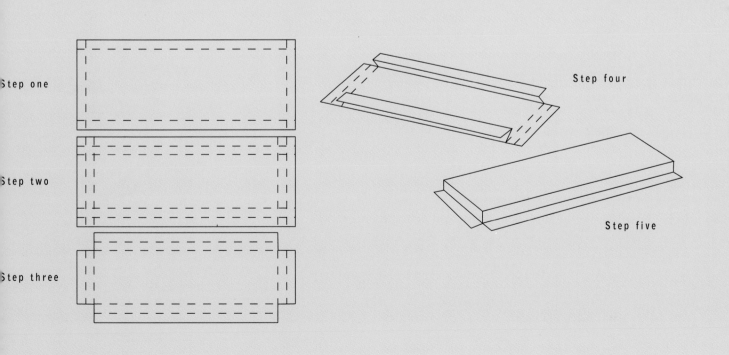

Step one

Step two

Step three

Step four

Step five

Seeded Center Flower Cards

When store-bought seeds are past their prime and you are ready to throw them out, use them to make textural centers for these ribbon-pierced flowers. Just about any leftover seeds can be used. Try small seeds, such as lettuce seeds or radish seeds. Garlic chive seeds (dark) and pepper seeds (light) are used in the illustrated cards.

INSTRUCTIONS

1. Photocopy the template onto card stock and cut out around the 4" (10.2 cm) square. Pierce the center dot of the template using a needle. Turn the paper over.

2. Place a strip of double-sided tape on the back of the 1¼" (3.2 cm) yellow circle. Remove the backing and adhere the circle to the center of the paper. Turn the paper over. Pierce the remaining dots on the circle template.

3. Thread the 36" (91 cm) length of organza ribbon onto the needle. Push the needle up from the back, through a dot on the template's inner circle. Pull the ribbon through, leaving a ribbon end of ½" (1.3 cm) on the other side. Push the needle and ribbon through the opposite dot of the outer circle. Pull the needle and ribbon through to the template side.

4. Push the needle and ribbon through the next dot on the outer circle and pull them through to the other side. Push the needle and ribbon through the opposite dot on the inner circle. Repeat the sewing steps until all twelve petals have been completed. Trim excess ribbon end to the length of ½" (1.3 cm).

MATERIALS

- weaving template (page 94)
- 1¼" (3.2 cm) yellow construction paper circle
- 36" (91 cm) length of ¾" (2 cm)-wide silk organza ribbon
- 6" (15.2 cm) length of ⅜" (1.3 cm)-wide silk organza ribbon
- 5½" x 8½" (14 cm x 21.6 cm) card stock
- 4" x 4" (10 cm x 10 cm) paper
- 3¼" x 3¼" (8.3 cm x 8.3 cm) tag board
- roll of ¼" (6 mm)-wide double-sided tape
- seeds
- needle
- white glue

HELPFUL HINT

The template can be enlarged or reduced to any size. The alternate design on page 33 was reduced to a 2½" (6.4 cm) circle and was sewn using a ⅜" (1 cm)-wide ribbon. The 1¼" (3.2 cm) yellow circle remained the same.

5. Place strips of double-sided tape along the edges of $3^{1}/_{4}$" x $3^{1}/_{4}$" (8.3 cm x 8.3 cm) tag board. With tape side up, center the tag board over the template side of the flower design. Remove the backing of the double-sided tape, and fold over and adhere the edges of the flower design onto the tape strips. Run another set of the double-sided tape strips along the edges of the square. Remove the backing paper.

6. Cut the 6" (15.2 cm) length of organza ribbon in half. Place ribbons on the diagonal in opposite corners of the flower design. Fold over the ribbon ends to the other side and adhere to the tape.

7. Fold the card stock in half. Center the flower design on the card stock and press down.

8. Fill the center of the flower with white glue. Sprinkle seeds into the glue. Shake off any excess seeds.

Trellis and Tendrils

Garden structures, such as trellises, provide necessary support as well as interesting architecture in the garden. The strong linear lines of the trellis and the curvy lines of the flowers give this card a bold geometric look.

INSTRUCTIONS

1. Cut the decorative paper into a $3\frac{1}{2}$" x $8\frac{1}{2}$" (8.9 cm x 21.6 cm) length. Along the short edges of the wrong side, run strips of double-sided tape. Turn the paper to the front. Lightly draw a line $\frac{1}{2}$" (1.3 cm) from the top and bottom edge of the short edges.

2. Cut the ribbon into three lengths of 9" (23 cm). Starting $\frac{3}{8}$" (1 cm) from the long edge of the paper, lay down one ribbon strip. Mark the ribbon's width on the top and bottom lines. Lay the ribbon down next to the pencil mark and mark the ribbon's width again. Repeat this step until there are six marks on each line.

3. On the bottom line, use a craft knife to cut a total of three lines, which lay between marks 1 and 2, 3 and 4, and 5 and 6. Slip the ribbon ends into the cuts. Turn the paper over and remove the tape backing. Secure the ribbon ends to the tape. Turn the paper over.

4. On the top line, cut an inverted "V" between marks 1 and 2, 3 and 4, and 5 and 6. Insert the ribbon ends into the cuts. Turn the paper over and remove the tape backing. Secure the ribbon ends to the tape. Turn the paper over.

5. Cut the remaining ribbon length in half. Run a length of tape along one edge of the ribbon. Remove the tape's backing. Reduce the ribbon's width by half by folding it in half lengthwise. Adhere the ribbon closed with the tape.

6. At the top, tuck the $\frac{1}{4}$" (6 mm) ribbon end behind the left side of the middle vertical ribbon. Cross over the center ribbon and weave the $\frac{1}{4}$" (6 mm) ribbon over and under the vertical ribbons. The $\frac{1}{4}$" (6 mm) ribbon should be angled downward in a zigzag manor when weaving. To finish, tuck the $\frac{1}{4}$" (6 mm) ribbon end under the left side of the middle ribbon.

MATERIALS

- 9" x $10\frac{3}{4}$" (22.9 cm x 27.3 cm) yellow, textured craft paper
- 6" x $8\frac{1}{2}$" (15.2 cm x 21.6 cm) decorative paper
- 50" (127 cm) length of $\frac{5}{8}$" (1.6 cm)-wide black ribbon
- roll of $\frac{1}{4}$" (6 mm)-wide double-sided tape
- nine assorted shapes of sequin flowers
- nine glass beads
- 36" (90 cm) length of craft wire
- bone folder
- scissors
- ruler
- pencil

7. Using the other ribbon length, repeat the design but in the other direction. Secure the ribbon ends behind the middle vertical ribbon. Using a bone folder, burnish the folds flat.

8. Cut five lengths of wire. Secure the flowers to the wire by inserting the wire from behind the flower, up through the hole. Slip a glass bead onto the wire and pass the wire back through the flower hole. Pull the ends tight. If the length of wire is long, put a flower sequin at the other end. Bend the wire into curves and slip it between the

ribbons. Continue creating flower vines with the remaining wire.

9. Remove the tape backing and adhere the trellis to the yellow craft paper, about $^1/_4$" (6 mm) from the edge. Fold over $^5/_8$" (1.6 cm) of the top and bottom edge of the yellow paper toward the trellis side. Next, fold the yellow paper in half approximately $^1/_4$" (6 mm) from the decorative paper's edge.

10. Run strips of tape along the long edges of the remaining piece of decorative paper. Adhere the paper to the inside of the card.

Teacup Card

If you grow herbs, such as chamomile, sage, or lemon mint, you can make your own tea for brewing. Dry a select group of herbs, package them into store bought tea bags, and send them off to a friend or two to warm themselves on a cold winter's day. Write a note of cheer or an herbal remedy associated with the tea on the hangtag.

INSTRUCTIONS

1. Copy the teacup template design onto white card stock. With right side up, cover the card stock paper with double-sided tape. Remove the backing. Place a 4" x 4" (10.2 cm x 10.2 cm) sheet of translucent paper over the teacup design, then cut it out. Copy the two oval shapes onto contrasting paper and cut them out.

2. Glue one oval to the bottom back of the teacup, as a saucer, and the other to the top back of the teacup, as the interior of the cup.

3. Using a craft knife, cut along the inside rim of the teacup, starting and ending $1/4$" (6 mm) from the outside edge. Slip the tag from behind the teacup and push it up and through the opening. If the tag does not fit through the opening, cut a little more along the rim until the opening is large enough to accommodate the tag's width. Remove the hangtag.

4. Stamp a one word greeting such as "enjoy" at the top of the tag.

5. Fold 12" (30.5 cm) of colored string in half. Slip the loop through the tag's grommet. Then slip the string's ends through the loop. Pull to tighten. Knot the ends and staple them to the tea bag.

MATERIALS

- 2½" x 5" (6.4 cm x 12.7 cm) hangtag
- 12" (30.5 cm) length of colored string
- 8½" x 11" (21.6 cm x 27.9 cm) white card stock
- 4" x 4" (10.2 cm x 10.2 cm) translucent paper
- 1¾" x 8" (4.4 cm x 20.3 cm) contrasting paper
- 4" x 12" (10.2 cm x 30.5 cm) purple embossed paper
- 6" x 8" (15.2 cm x 20.3 cm) sheet of double-sided tape
- teacup template (page 95)
- oval template (page 95)
- tea bag
- small alphabet letter stamps
- craft knife
- stapler
- glue

6. Fold the 4" x 12" (10.2 cm x 30.5 cm) embossed paper in half. Open the paper. Run a small length of double-sided tape on the top back of the teacup. Remove the backing and adhere the teacup to the bottom half of the embossed paper. Slip the tag through the teacup opening.

Chapter 3

Photo Cards:
The Garden Within the Viewfinder

As any avid gardener knows, fleeting beauty is one of the garden's most powerful messages. With the luck of good weather and healthy soil, each bud will open. Each sprout will grow into its ideal form and then begin its decline. With the drama of variable light, the garden may start the day as soft, misty drifts, then, at high noon change into patterns of bright colors and shapes, and finally at dusk, yield into purple shadows of nightfall. With the change of seasons, there will always be first snowfalls, beautiful rainbows, and delightful animal visitations.

To immortalize the beauty of a moment—when light, color, and story come together—the gardener may capture her vision with a camera. For the scientific-minded, there are photos that record such things as plant development. Other photos are used for a seasonal review and next year's garden planning. And then, there are those wonderful, special photographs that can offer a message of personal growth, renewal, and love.

Over time, the gardener's personal quest will yield an impressive collection of photos. Throughout the year, you may want to share this bounty of the garden and the beauty of the moment with your friends and relatives. This is your opportunity to enchant them with your special photographs.

The following projects are designed to give you the opportunity to enhance your photo collection and to create photo keepsakes to treasure or give away to others.

Decorated Photo Corner Frame

Create an elegant frame for garden photos with a contemporary twist on the old-fashioned photo corner theme. A variety of stamped or transfer designs can be used to create decorative corners. Metallic inks work nicely to add a delicate sheen to the final frame design.

INSTRUCTIONS

1. Using a bone folder and ruler, measure, then score a line 2$\frac{1}{2}$" (6.4 cm) from each short edge of the translucent paper.

2. Fold up each 2$\frac{1}{2}$" (6.4 cm) section at the score lines to create panels. Position the paper horizontally with the panels folding up and toward the center of the paper.

3. Rub one triangular transfer or stamp a triangular motif in each corner of folded panels. Place the designs $\frac{1}{16}$" (1.6 mm) away from the edges of the paper.

4. Open the panels flat. For each corner, cut an opening $\frac{1}{16}$" (1.6 mm) outside of the stamp or transfer's diagonal line, beginning and ending $\frac{1}{16}$" (1.6 mm) from the fold and the edge of the paper.

5. Fold panels over again and slip the corners of a 4" x 6" (10.2 cm x 15.2 cm) photo into the openings.

MATERIALS

- 11" x 4$\frac{1}{4}$" (27.9 cm x 10.8 cm) colored translucent paper
- triangular transfer or rubber stamp (shown here: Chartpak transfers, Victorian lace, silver)
- silver ink pad (if using a stamp)
- transparent ruler
- craft knife
- bone folder

HELPFUL HINT

If the diagonal cut that holds the photo in place is accidentally broken, repair with a small piece of transparent tape from behind. Trim away excess tape.

 GOING ONE STEP FURTHER

For an element of intrigue when you present your photo frame, create a paper band, 2³/₄" x 8¹/₂" (7 cm x 21.6 cm) to partially screen the photo. Slip the decorated band between the paper and the back of the photo. Then fold each end of the band over the photo. Adhere the band closed with a sticker.

 GOING ONE STEP FURTHER

Want to add a personal message? Punch a hole in a small tag, add your greeting, and thread it onto the ribbon strand before looping the ribbons together.

$\mathcal{V}$ictorian Locket Photo Holder

This photo project is based on the locket—a small, ornamental case designed to hold a cherished photo or keepsake. Slip one of your favorite photos under the locket tabs. Then link the two lockets together with metallic threads and mail to a special friend.

INSTRUCTIONS

1. Lightly mark the center points of the short edges of the translucent paper. With a pencil, lightly draw a line between these two points, dividing the paper in half.

2. Center the transfer or stamped image on this line with each design positioned about $\frac{1}{8}$" (3 mm) from the opposite ends of the paper. Adhere the transfer following the manufacturer's instructions or apply your stamped design.

3. Next, lightly draw a line parallel to and 2" (5 cm) inside of each short edge, skipping over the stamped image.

4. Using a craft knife, cut along the edge of the design that extends past this drawn line into the center section of the paper. Slip a 4" x 6" (10.2 cm x 15.2 cm) photo under the cut area of the locket.

5. Using a punch, make a hole through one end of the locket and the photo. To create a link between lockets, thread the ends of the 18" (46 cm) length of ribbon up through card holes to the front. Loop the ribbons around each other in the center, and then return each ribbon end back through its original hole. Adhere the ribbon ends to the back of the card using stickers.

$\mathscr{B}$ee Happy Photo Card

This folded card creates a stagelike setting for a favorite garden photo. The photo is the backdrop and the bees the main characters. The recipient of this charming, freestanding card will want to display it where it will receive rave reviews.

MATERIALS

- 4" x 10" (10.2 cm x 25.4 cm) medium weight decorative paper
- bee template (page 96)
- 4" x 6" (10.2 cm x 15.2 cm) photo, landscape format
- roll of ¼" (6 mm)-wide double-sided tape
- pencil
- ruler
- craft knife
- bone folder

HELPFUL HINT

If you prefer not to use the original 4" x 6" (10.2 cm x 15.2 cm) photo, use a color photocopy instead.

INSTRUCTIONS

1. With the paper right side up, measure 2" (5 cm) in from each short edge of the paper, and draw two parallel pencil lines.

2. Photocopy, then cut out the bee template from a piece of yellow card stock. Adhere a strip of double-sided tape to the wrong side of each bumblebee. Position the bumblebee's wings within the 2" (5 cm)-wide panel. Antennas and stinger should extend beyond the panel on both sides. Remove the tape backing and adhere each bee in the correct position.

3. Using a craft knife, cut along the bumblebee's stinger, beginning and ending at the pencil line. Fold the panels toward the back of the card along the pencil line. Turn the card over, keeping the panels folded back.

4. Run doubled-sided tape along the top and bottom of the photograph. Center and adhere the photo in the middle section of the card.

5. Using a bone folder and ruler, score a line on the photo, which measures 1¼" (3.2 cm) from each folded edge. Fold along the scored line, returning bumblebee panels to the front of the card.

Garden Gate Greeting

At the garden gate, an opportunity full of promise and wonder awaits. Crossing over the threshold, you can wander along the garden paths, marveling over each and every flower that catches your eye. Designed as a simple paper cut out, let your recipient open the gate onto a beautiful garden photograph.

INSTRUCTIONS

1. Cut a 6" x 8½" (15.2 cm x 21.6 cm) section from the card stock. Fold it in half.

2. Stamp the floral design onto the remaining 5" x 8½" (12.7 cm x 21.6 cm) section of card stock. Sprinkle with embossing powder. Apply heat with the heat gun to melt the powder.

3. Trace the contour of the garden gate template onto the stamped paper. Using a craft knife, cut out the design. Cut the design into two pieces by cutting along the left side of the gate.

4. On the back of the last picket of each unit, run a strip of double-sided tape.

5. Place the two picket units on the photograph, lining up the bottom edges. The left unit should extend one picket under the gate picket. Fold over the extra pickets, which extend beyond the photograph edges to the back of the photograph. Remove the tape backing and adhere.

6. On the back of the photograph, run a strip of double-sided tape along the top and bottom. Remove the tape's backing and adhere to the front of the folded card stock.

7. Adhere the butterfly onto the first picket of the garden gate. Fold the wings up.

MATERIALS

- garden gate template (page 97)
- 4" x 6" (10.2 cm x 15.2 cm) photograph
- 8½" x 11" (21.6 cm x 27.9 cm) off-white card stock
- 1½" (3.8 cm) paper butterfly cut out
- embossing powder, clear
- roll of ¼" (6 mm)-wide double-sided tape
- floral design rubber stamp
- light green ink pad
- heat gun
- craft knife
- ruler

$\mathcal{G}$arden Silhouettes

MATERIALS

- 7$\frac{1}{8}$" x 11" (18.1 cm x 27.9 cm) colored paper
- silhouette-style clip art or other black and white art
- plastic window decal sheet (shown here: Avery window decals #3276)
- 4" x 6" (10.2 cm x 15.2 cm) photo
- blank greeting cards & envelopes (shown here: Strathmore KIDS Series)
- ribbon or paper ribbon
- roll of $\frac{1}{4}$" (6 mm)-wide double-sided tape
- craft knife
- transparent ruler
- paper punch
- needle
- ink-jet printer

Close-up shots of flowers and vegetables make great fantasy backdrops for cut paper silhouettes. The illustrated silhouettes were transferred to decal sheets using an ink-jet printer. Decals stick to photos and are easily removed and replaced without causing harm to the photos.

INSTRUCTIONS

1. Transfer the silhouette design to the decal sheet using an ink-jet printer. Position the decal over the photo and adhere. Trim excess decal from the edges using a craft knife. On the back of the photo, place strips of double-sided tape along the top and bottom.

2. Fold the colored paper in half. Unfold. Center the photo on one half of the paper. Use a needle to mark the four corners of the photo by piercing the paper. Remove the photo. To create the window opening, cut an area that is $\frac{1}{8}$" (3 mm) greater than the photo markings using the craft knife and a transparent ruler.

3. Place the blank card inside the folded colored paper and clip the papers together. Open the card. On the fold, use a needle to pierce three tiny holes denoting the center, 1" (2.5 cm) from the top edge, and 1" (2.5 cm) from the bottom edge. Use a paper punch to create $\frac{1}{8}$" (3 mm) holes.

4. Thread a paper ribbon through the holes and tie a bow on the outside of the card.

5. On the blank card, position the photo within the window opening. Remove the tape backing and adhere.

HELPFUL HINT

If you don't have access to a computer, your local printer can transfer your silhouette design to a transparency. Be sure to tell the printer that the black design needs to be opaque. The transparency can then be adhered to the back of the card window to create the same effect.

Movable Cards

Flowers in Motion

There is a life force flowing through nature. The sun illuminates and the plants grow. The rain comes down and nourishment is taken up. Honeybees buzz, aspen leaves flutter, pine branches sway, flower buds open, ripe seeds fall. The garden is energized with continuous movement, change, and flux. Re-create the magic with the enchantment of energized garden greetings that pop up, swirl, and unfold. Engaging and intriguing, these projects bring alive the power of the wind, the mystery of growth, and the motion of flowers unfolding.

Projects allow recipients to:

- *Unfold a flower to reveal a hidden message*

- *Open a card with whimsical pop-up posies*

- *Spread out a fan and behold a bouquet*

- *Gather seeds to cultivate in the future*

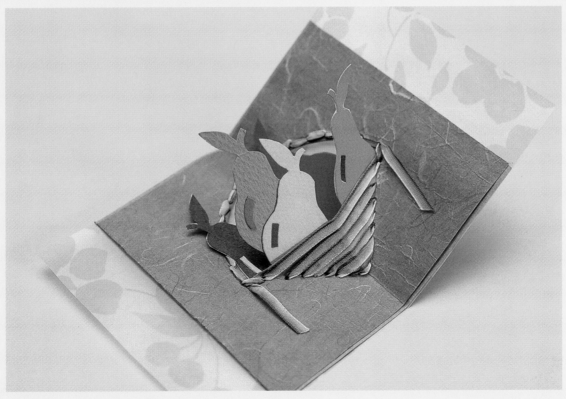

Flutter Bug Origami Greeting

MATERIALS

- 4$\frac{1}{2}$" x 9" (11.4 cm x 22.9 cm) medium weight paper
- large motif stamp
- flower stamp
- butterfly stamp
- blue, yellow, and red ink pads
- craft knife
- bone folder
- pencil
- ruler

HELPFUL HINT

For critical placement of the butterfly stamp on the centerline, place a dot on the stamp's edge using an indelible marker, marking the top and bottom centerline of the butterfly design. Use these marks to position the stamp on the centerline. A right angle ruler can also be helpful in proper placement.

The card's size can be amended with a 2:1 proportion of length to width: 11" x 5$\frac{1}{2}$" (28 cm x 14 cm), 18" x 9" (46 cm x 23 cm), etc.

What can be more delightful to the gardener's eye than the graceful journey of a butterfly flitting from flower to flower? After alighting on a bloom, it sips nectar while its wings gently open and close. This card's geometric design simulates the butterfly's triangular shape, while the folding and unfolding patterns mimic the movement of the wings. Feel free to write a bright and cheerful note along an imaginary curving line, expressive of the butterfly's serendipitous flight through the garden.

INSTRUCTIONS

1. Score the centerline to divide the paper into two squares. Score four diagonal lines dividing the two squares into eight triangles; the lines create an "X" in each square. Find and mark the center point of the centerline by placing a ruler along the two points of intersection where the diagonals meet.

2. Stamp a butterfly exactly on the centerline and center point. Stamp a decorative motif around the butterfly using other stamps. Using a craft knife, cut along the outline of the wings only, leaving the body and antennas uncut along the fold line.

3. With the paper horizontal on your work surface, take the lower left corner and match it with the top point of the centerline, creasing along the scored diagonal. Take the upper right corner and match it with the bottom point of the centerline, creasing gently along the scored diagonal line. Take the lower left corner and match it with the top point of the centerline. Take the top right corner and match it with the bottom of the centerline. You should have a folded piece of paper in the shape of a square.

4. Unfold the paper and repeat directions starting with step 3, except this time, fold the butterfly wings upward and perpendicular to the paper while folding. Fold the wings down flat against the square to present the card.

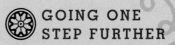 **GOING ONE STEP FURTHER**

The card can be tied shut with the aid of an 8" (20 cm) length of $1/8$" (3 mm)-wide silk ribbon. After completing step 4, fold the square along the centerline to create a triangular shape. With the butterfly wings out and away from the fold, mark a point $1/4$" (6 mm) away from and just below the butterfly's abdomen. Center this point within the paper punch's opening and cut a hole through all of the card layers. Fold the ribbon in half and slip the loop through the hole. With the loop placed at the butterfly's head, pull the ribbon ends through the loop. Tie a bow at the butterfly's head to mimic the look of antennas.

Pop-up Potted Posies

In late winter, gardening catalogs arrive almost everyday in the mail. While perusing those beautiful catalogs, select a few beautiful photos and make one or two pop-up greeting cards. Also, if you order bulbs or other plantings to give as gifts, this is a great card to give to the recipient. The card will illustrate nicely what she has to look forward to come spring and summer.

INSTRUCTIONS

1. Score a parallel line 2" (5.1 cm) from the 6" (15.2 cm)-long edge of the blue paper. Crease along the scored line. Unfold the paper and lay flat.

2. Along the fold line, mark dots at the following six locations starting from the left edge: $^5/_8$" (1.6 cm), $1^5/_8$" (4.1 cm), $2^3/_8$" (6 cm), $3^3/_8$" (8.6 cm), $4^3/_8$" (11 cm), and $5^3/_8$" (13.7 cm).

3. Draw three pairs of parallel lines centered on the fold line. The first pair consists of 2" (5.1 cm) lines at the $^5/_8$" (1.6 cm) and $1^5/_8$" (4.1 cm) marks. The second pair consists of $2^1/_2$" (6.4 cm) lines at the $2^3/_8$" (6 cm) and $3^3/_8$" (8.6 cm) marks. The third pair consists of 2" (5.1 cm) lines at the $4^3/_8$" (11 cm) and $5^3/_8$" (13.7 cm) marks. Using a craft knife, cut all six lines.

4. Turn the blue paper over. Run a strip of double-sided tape along the two 6" (15.2 cm)-long edges.

5. Turn the paper over. Place the blue paper over the yellow vellum with $^1/_4$" (6 mm) of vellum extending beyond the blue paper's top. Remove the tape's backing. Adhere the sheets together.

6. Fold the paper at a 90° angle. Reverse the folds of the three 1" (2.5 cm)-wide strips. They should look like tables jutting out. The flowerpots will be attached to these three strips. Flatten paper.

MATERIALS

- three 2" (5.1 cm) square catalog blooms
- 4" x 6" (10.2 cm x 15.2 cm) metallic copper card stock
- 24" (61 cm) length of $^3/_8$" (1 cm)-wide ribbon
- $5^3/_4$" x 6" (14.6 cm x 15.2 cm) blue paper
- $6^1/_2$" x 6" (16.5 cm x 15.2 cm) yellow vellum paper
- roll of $^1/_4$" (6 mm)-wide double-sided tape
- 4" x 6" (10.2 cm x 15.2 cm) sheet of double-sided tape
- flowerpot template (page 98)
- craft knife
- bone folder
- ruler
- white glue

HELPFUL HINT

The card can be mailed either flat or folded. Include a brief description to the recipient on how to pop up her flowers if mailing flat. A simple description would be: Fold your card at a 90° angle and enjoy!

7. Cut the metallic paper into three 4" x 2" (10.2 cm x 5.1 cm) strips. Trace the flowerpot shape at the bottom of each copper paper strip. Adhere the catalog blooms onto the sheet of double-sided tape. Using a craft knife, cut out the blooms. Cut one side of bloom to have a flat edge. This edge will be placed on the traced flowerpot rim. If preferred, a petal can overlap the rim, so trim accordingly.

8. Remove the tape's backing from the blooms. Adhere the blooms to the metallic paper with the flat side at the flowerpot rim. Using a craft knife, cut along the outline of the potted blooms.

9. Run a strip of double-sided tape down the middle of the bottom half of the three 1" (2.5 cm) strips. Remove the backing. With the bottom of the pots lined up with the bottom fold of the 1" (2.5 cm) strips, adhere the flowerpots to each strip.

10. Fold the card at a 90° angle, easing the flowerpots to stand up and away from the blue paper. Cut the ribbon into three 8" (20 cm) lengths. Tie each length into a bow. Glue each bow at the bottom corner of each pot on the blue paper.

$\mathscr{B}$ouquet Fanfare

Unfold a rainbow of colors with this bouquet of bright and sassy zinnias. Each panel of the fan can be ornamented with a letter of your message, such as T-H-A-N-K-U or M-I-S-S-Y-O-U.

INSTRUCTIONS

1. On a copy machine, reproduce the flower panel on medium weight paper six times.

2. Hand color each panel as desired.

3. Stack the flower panels together and clip with a binder clip. Punch a $^3/_{16}$" (4.8 mm) hole at the bottom of the fan.

4. Set an eyelet in the hole.

5. With the panels stacked together, pierce a hole through all panels using an awl at the center/top of the fan about $^1/_2$" (1.3 cm) from the edge.

6. Open the fan. Begin sewing from the back. Pull the needle and thread through to the front of the first panel. Then loop the thread over the top edge and return to the back of the panel. Secure the ends with a knot. Return the thread to the front by passing the needle through the hole. Position the second panel with a slight overlap over the first panel. Push the needle and thread through the back of the second panel to the front. Then loop over the top edge, push the needle and thread from the back to the front again. Position the third panel with a slight overlap of the second panel. Repeat the sewing sequence until all panels have been tied together. Tie off the threads to the back of the last panel.

7. Slip the ribbon through the eyelet and pull it through until the ribbon has equal amounts on either side of the eyelet. Slip one end through the eyelet again and pull.

MATERIALS

- flower panel template (page 98)
- $^3/_{16}$" (4.8 mm) paper punch
- 18" (46 cm) length of ribbon
- 36" (92 cm) length of thread
- $^3/_{16}$" (4.8 mm) eyelet
- eyelet punch
- needle
- awl
- binder clip
- colored markers

HELPFUL HINT

Be sure to check the thickness of the stacked panels against the depth of the eyelet being used. Too many panels will cause the eyelet to malfunction and the fan to fall apart. If a large number of panels are desired, use an album post to secure the panels together.

⚜ GOING ONE STEP FURTHER

While the fan is spread out, turn the card over and write a message or note on the back. Also a very simple message such as "THANK U" can be revealed during the unfolding of the fan. Simply stamp individual letters onto each flower disk spelling out a greeting. The example on the right has the addition of two, nonlettered panels: one at the beginning and the other at the end with a total of eight panels.

Fruit Basket Pop-Up

This greeting card delivers a bountiful harvest. Create a pretty, hand-woven ribbon basket and fill it with rainbow-colored pears. The fruit collection pops up into view when the card is opened. When placed on a shelf, the shapely forms stay fresh for a very long time.

MATERIALS

- 5" x 12" (12.7 cm x 30.5 cm) card stock
- 5" x 8½" (12.7 cm x 21.6 cm) decorative paper
- five cut out paper fruits, approximately 2½" (6.4 cm) high
- 1 yard (90 cm) of ¼" (6 mm)-wide ribbon
- roll of ¼" (6 mm)-wide double-sided tape
- 1/16" (1.5 mm) paper punch
- craft knife
- needle
- ruler
- hammer
- compass
- bone folder
- scissors
- pencil

INSTRUCTIONS

1. Fold the card stock into quarters. Unfold and lay the paper flat. On the last fold, place a ruler and make a pencil mark 2½" (6.4 cm) and 1¼" (3.2 cm) from the bottom. Draw a 3½" (8.9 cm)-long line centering it on the 2½" (6.4 cm) mark, parallel to the bottom edge. Using a bone folder, score two lines connecting the end points of the 3½" (8.9 cm) line to the 1¼" (3.2 cm) mark. Place a compass point on the 2½" (6.4 cm) mark. Open the compass until it reaches the end of the 3½" (8.9 cm) line. Draw a half circle above the triangle. Using a craft knife, cut along the 3½" (8.9 cm) line. Next, reverse the fold of the triangle by pulling down the cut edge of the triangle while pressing down on the scored lines. Fold closed along the fold line. Open.

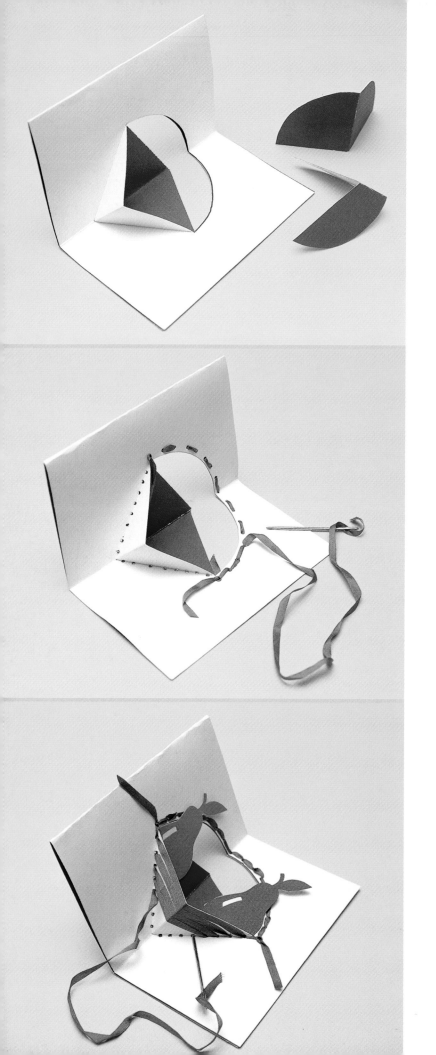

2. Fold the paper in half with the drawing side up. Using a craft knife, cut along the circle line, cutting through both paper layers. Remove the half circle shape from the top layer. In the half circle area, place a ruler on the fold and mark 1" (2.5 cm) up from circle's center. Using a craft knife, cut two lines, each radiating down from the 1" (2.5 cm) mark to each of the half circle's corners. Remove the shape. Place a strip of double-sided tape on the inside edge of one of the short sides. Remove the backing and adhere to sides.

3. Using a paper punch, punch out seventeen holes along the outside edge of the circle. Next, punch out eight holes on each scored line of the triangle. Fold the ribbon in half and cut into two pieces. Take one piece and cut it in half. Thread a needle with a short length of ribbon. Begin on the right side of the card and weave the ribbon through the holes of the basket handle. The weaving will look like a broken line. To complete the weaving of the handle, thread the other short ribbon onto the needle and begin weaving from the other end of the basket handle.

4. Place one fruit in each corner of the basket. Re-punch the holes, making new holes through the paper fruit. Place a 2" (5 cm) strip of double-sided tape to the top edge of the triangle. Remove the backing. Thread the needle with the long length of ribbon. Begin weaving the basket from the back side of the card, coming up through the first hole and going to the opposite side of the basket, and passing the needle and ribbon through hole number two. From the back, come up through the third hole, just below the last hole, across the basket to its opposite side. Continue weaving back and forth until the basket is complete. To be sure the weaving is done correctly, the back side of the card should have a broken line of ribbon along the two scored lines.

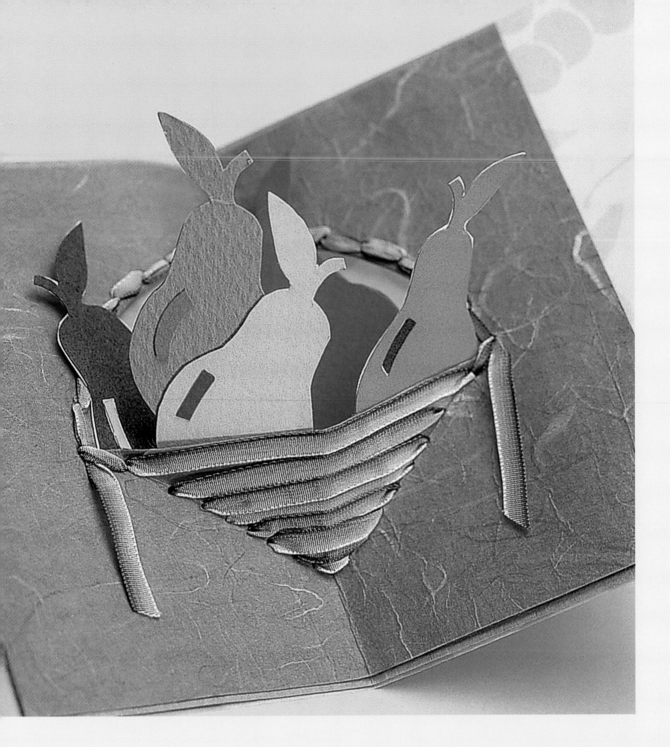

5. Arrange the remaining paper fruits in the basket.
   They can be placed either to the inside back of
   the basket or to the inside front of the basket.
   The fruits should be positioned to either side of
   the fold. The card will only close properly if the
   pieces are not placed directly on the fold. Test
   their positioning before taping by folding the card
   in half and observing how the paper fruits fall
   into position when the card is closed. Use double-
   sided tape to adhere the pieces in place. Fold the
   decorative paper in half and attach to the back of
   the pop-up card using strips of double-sided tape.

HELPFUL HINT

When adhering two boards together with double-sided tape, begin by lightly cutting a line through the tape backing, approximately 1" (2.5 cm) from an edge. Do not remove backing material. Put the two surfaces together, lining up the sides. Attach a binder clip to the bottom, opposite the cut line. Separate the boards slightly at the top and remove the 1" (2.5 cm)-wide backing strip from the double-sided tape. Adhere the boards together. Remove the binder clip. Slightly separate the boards at the bottom and remove the remaining backing. Adhere the boards together. Using this technique, it is far easier to take the boards apart if they need to be realigned.

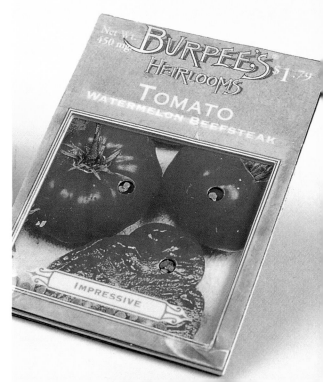

$\mathcal{S}$eed Packet Game

MATERIALS

- front of 4^1/$_2$" x 3^1/$_4$" (11.4 cm x 8.3 cm) seed packet
- fifteen seeds
- 4^1/$_2$" x 3^1/$_4$" (11.4 cm x 8.3 cm) piece of clear acetate
- two 4^1/$_2$" x 3^1/$_4$" (1.4 cm x 8.3 cm) pieces of mat board (one marked A, one marked B)
- 4^1/$_2$" x 3^1/$_4$" (11.4 cm x 8.3 cm) colored paper
- 10" x 10" (25 cm x 25 cm) sheet of double-sided tape
- ^{3}/$_{16}$" (4.8 mm) paper punch
- mat knife

Turn a collection of beautiful seed packets into pocket games for children. While playing these simple games, children can visually associate a particular vegetable with its seed. Also, the games are great illustrations, demonstrating the wide variety of seed shapes and sizes. For adults, the game cards become handsome shadow boxes when placed on a shelf.

INSTRUCTIONS

1. Place double-sided tape on the back of the seed packet, on both sides of mat board A, and on one side of mat board B.

2. Cut a 2^1/$_2$" x 2^1/$_2$" (6.4 cm x 6.4 cm) area from the seed packet, which highlights the vegetable or flower.

3. Trace the opening of the seed packet on mat board A and on the untaped side of mat board B. Using a mat knife, cut out the marked area from mat board A only.

4. Adhere the acetate to the back of the seed packet. Adhere the acetate and seed packet panel to mat board A.

5. Remove the backing from the 2^1/$_2$" x 2^1/$_2$" (6.4 cm x 6.4 cm) seed packet illustration and adhere to mat board B within the area previously traced.

6. Using the paper punch, punch out three or four holes within the seed packet illustration. Adhere the colored paper to the back of mat board B.

7. Place seeds into the holes.

8. Remove the tape backing from mat board A and adhere it to mat board B.

Posy Packets

These six-sided bundles hold a surprise greeting. As each petal is unfolded, a hand-stamped note is revealed within the flower's interior. And with a few twists of the elastic band, the cheery posy can bloom and reign on the end of a pencil.

INSTRUCTIONS

1. Trace the posy template shape onto the plain side of the paper. Stamp your message multiple times on the paper surface. Cut out the flower shape.

2. Place the colored paper circle in the center of the flower. Punch a hole through both pieces of paper. Insert and set the eyelet in the hole.

3. Fold the elastic cord in half and tie an overhand knot at the ends. With printed side up, slip the loop down through the eyelet opening and pull the elastic knot up against the eyelet.

4. Close the flower by folding over each petal, one on top of the other. Secure the bundle by slipping the elastic loop over the closed form.

MATERIALS

- 5" x 5" (12.7 cm x 12.7 cm) decorative paper
- 1¹⁄₂" (3.8 cm)-wide color circle
- 6" (15 cm)-long metallic gold elastic cord
- ¹⁄₄" (6 mm) paper punch
- ¹⁄₄" (6 mm) eyelet
- posy template (page 99)
- eyelet setter
- small letter stamping blocks
- ink pads
- hammer
- ruler
- craft knife
- scissors

HELPFUL HINT

To stamp a word instead of individual letters, group the stamps side by side and tape them together. If you would like the word to appear in an arc, hold the grouping in your fingers in a curved position while stamping. If a word has a letter appearing twice, such as the word "soon," and you have only one letter available, place any letter block upside down to hold the space open while printing. Later, remove the needed letter from the grouping and stamp it in the open space.

$\mathcal{K}$oi Fish Pond

MATERIALS

- two 6" x 6" (15.2 cm x 15.2 cm) pieces of thin cardboard
- 6" x 6" (15.2 cm x 15.2 cm) decorative origami paper
- three 6" x 6" (15.2 cm x 15.2 cm) foil origami papers
- 6" x 6" (15.2 cm x 15.2 cm) clear contact paper
- 6" x 6" (15.2 cm x 15.2 cm) sheet of double-sided tape
- fish stickers
- tassel
- four tiny paper brads
- three $\frac{1}{4}$" (6 mm) foam sticky squares
- compass
- $\frac{1}{8}$" (3 mm) paper punch
- craft knife
- scissors
- ruler

HELPFUL HINT

The tricky part of this project is positioning the pinwheels so they'll rotate when the sticky squares come in contact with the blades. The squares push the pinwheels into rotation when the circle is rotated by hand.

Energize this water garden greeting card with twirling pinwheels and whirling fish, by spinning the inner circle. In Chinese culture, the fish symbolizes wealth and success. Write your well wishes on the back of this movable card and mail it to a friend for the start of the New Year or a new planting season.

INSTRUCTIONS

1. Place a sheet of double-sided tape on the back of the decorative origami paper. Mark the center of the paper. Place the point of the compass on the center mark and draw a 4" (10.2 cm)-wide circle. Using a craft knife, cut out the circle. Adhere the paper circle to one of the square cardboard pieces. Cut out the circle and cover it with the clear contact paper. Trim away the excess contact paper. Arrange the fish stickers on the circle. Place the three $\frac{1}{4}$" (6 mm) sticky squares near the edge of the circle, dividing the circle into thirds.

2. Adhere the decorative paper with the circular hole onto the other cardboard square. Turn the square over, wrong side up. Draw a $1\frac{1}{8}"$ (2.9 cm) square in each corner of the cardboard. Punch a hole in the corner of each small square that is nearest the center of the board. Turn the square over, right side up. Insert the tassel into one of the corner holes.

3. Position the fish circle within the circular area of the cardboard square. Place the paper punch on the compass point, mark and cut through the two boards. Insert a paper brad in the hole.

4. To make the pinwheels, cut three $2\frac{5}{8}"$ (6.7 cm) squares from the origami paper. Stack the paper squares and pierce through all layers at the center with the compass point. Cut a diagonal line from each corner to the center, stopping about a $\frac{1}{8}"$ (3 mm) from the center point. Fold every other paper point to the center of the square. With the point of the craft knife, make a tiny center cut through all layers. Pass a paper brad through the cut.

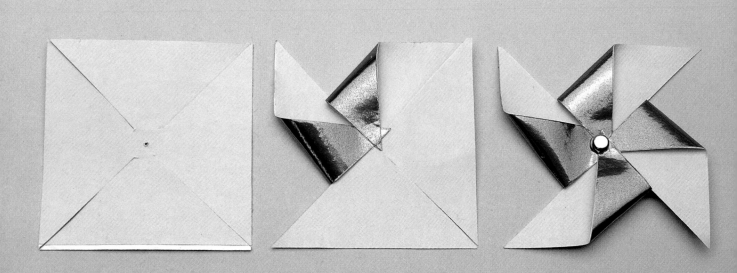

5. Place the pinwheel's paper brad through a corner hole of the decorative square. Fasten it to the back of the board. Repeat this step with the two remaining origami squares. Check to see if all pinwheels rotate easily before rotating the inner circle.

 **GOING ONE STEP FURTHER**

If you like double-sided colored paper for the pinwheels, adhere two sheets together using a sheet of double-sided tape.

Chapter 5

Special Occasion Cards:

With Every Leaf a Miracle

New life, life in motion, always evolving, life ending.

We observe transitions and passages, growth and renewal, through rituals and celebrations that enrich our lives throughout the year. There is a strong desire to honor, sanctify, and memorialize these momentous events and to bring special attention to special occasions. We feel connected with others and our world when we take part in customs that enable us to express appreciation, celebration, generosity, comfort, and foremost, love. Bless these celebratory events through the generous act of creating a very special card. Make your card one of lasting endurance, because special occasions create special memories that are treasured over and over again.

- *Herald a life passage with a flight of birds making their way to their new abode*

- *Celebrate continual growth and renewal with the upward curve of flower petals in an iris bouquet.*

- *Illuminate a special event, such as a wedding, through the creation of a paper lantern card*

$\mathcal{L}$adybug Invite

One grand ladybug sits upon a leaf, while her many neighbors wander in all directions. The leaf slips out from under her and opens to reveal a handwritten message: "Let's get together soon, away from the business of daily life." Easily adapted for any occasion, this card makes a great summer party invite too!

MATERIALS

- twenty-five small ladybug stickers
- two large ladybug stickers
- 8" x 5$\frac{1}{2}$" (20.3 cm x 14 cm) white medium weight paper
- 7$\frac{1}{2}$" x 5" (19.1 cm x 12.7 cm) green medium weight paper
- leaf template (page 100)
- craft knife
- ruler

HELPFUL HINT

If you need many invitations, have color copies made of the small ladybug arrangement. Then proceed with step 2.

INSTRUCTIONS

1. Make a random arrangement of twenty-five ladybug stickers on white paper.

2. Measure the large ladybug body, not including the length of antennas. With this measurement, cut a straight line at an angle anywhere in the middle of the white paper. Cut another line, parallel to previous cut, approximately $\frac{1}{32}$" (.8 mm) apart.

3. Take both large ladybug stickers and fold in half. Unfold. Remove the right antenna of one and the left from the other. Turn the stickers over. Using the craft knife, gently cut just the paper backing of stickers along the fold line. Fold in half again.

4. Ease one half of the ladybug sticker (the side without an antenna) through the cut of the white paper. Repeat with the remaining sticker. Turn the paper over. Remove the sticker backing and adhere to the back of the paper.

5. Trace the leaf template onto the green paper and cut it out. Along its outline, fold in half.

6. Use the craft knife to cut two parallel lines, approximately $\frac{1}{16}$" (1.6 mm) apart, down the leaf's center. The line length equals the length of the ladybug as measured in step 2.

7. Write a message on the inside of the leaf. Close the leaf and slide it under the ladybug.

Cut Flowers for a Special Couple

In Europe during the eighteenth century, there was a system invented by Lady Mary Montague called the Language of Flowers. It was a list associating flowers with romantic and heartfelt meanings. For instance, the rose had the meaning of love, the daisy was innocence, and the ivy symbolized fidelity. Someone sending a bouquet of flowers to a lover or dear friend could communicate intimate or sentimental feelings to the other.

In this card, the two golden irises send a beautiful "message" of happiness to a very special couple celebrating their fiftieth wedding anniversary.

INSTRUCTIONS

1. Trim a 1¼" x 11" (3.2 cm x 27.9 cm) strip from the dark gold metallic paper. Fold the larger sheet in half.

2. Lightly stamp the corners of the maroon paper with the flower design. Sprinkle with embossing powder. Apply heat with a heat gun to melt the powder.

3. Place the stencil on the paper and dab the ink in the open areas. Wipe the stencil clean and turn it over. Position the turned over stencil in an open area and dab with the copper color.

4. Using a craft knife, cut along the stenciled lines, but leave a hinged area so the petals and leaves are still attached in places. Bend, curl, or lift the flowers and leaves creating a three-dimensional look.

5. Turn the paper over and run strips of tape along the edges. Remove the tape's backing and adhere the paper to the light gold paper. Turn the paper

MATERIALS

- 8½" x 11" (21.6 cm x 28 cm) dark gold metallic card stock
- 5⅜" x 6" (13.7 cm x 15.2 cm) light gold metallic paper
- 5⅞" x 5¼" (14.9 cm x 13.3 cm) maroon card stock
- roll of ¼" (6 mm)-wide double-sided tape
- three ¼" (6 mm) sticky squares
- 5" (12.7 cm) iris stencil
- flower stamp
- colonial blue ink pad
- champagne and copper metallic ink daubers
- gold embossing powder
- heat gun
- craft knife

over and run strips of tape along the paper edges. Remove the tape's backing and place it $^7/_8$" (2.2 mm) from the bottom of the dark metallic paper.

6. Draw the numbers "5" and "0" on the strip of dark metallic paper. Using a craft knife, cut out the numbers. Adhere two sticky squares to the back of the "5." Adhere one sticky square to the bottom right of the "0." Adhere the numbers to the upper right corner of the maroon paper, slightly overlapping the "5" over the "0."

7. In the space below the irises, hand cut stencil-like letters for the card's message. Stamping small block letters is another method for creating the card's message.

Chinese Paper Lantern Card

MATERIALS

- 9" x 12" (23.9 cm x 30.5 cm) maroon paper

- two 4¼" x 11" (10.8 cm x 27.9 cm) pieces of decorative paper

- four 2½" (6.4 cm) square pieces of translucent paper

- 18" (46 cm) length of 1½" (3.8 cm)-wide ribbon

- six marsh reed stems

- compass

- roll of ¼" (6 mm)-wide double-sided tape

- two 3" x 5" (7.5 cm x 12.5 cm) sheets of double-sided tape

- craft knife

- glue

HELPFUL HINT

It will be necessary to flatten the card before slipping it into an envelope. If you would like to mail this card, reduce the lantern's length to fit a 4¾" x 11" (12.1 cm x 27.9 cm) business size envelope.

In the summer, garden lanterns are bright, dancing illuminations, swaying in a gentle breeze. For a newly wedded couple, this specialized card lights up the good fortunes you're sending their way. Designed as a small table lantern, a small votive can be placed within the opened center. The light shining through the portals will dance like a full moon in a bamboo grove.

INSTRUCTIONS

1. Fold the maroon paper in half. Unfold the paper. Fold the paper in half in the other direction. Fold the paper in half one more time. Unfold the paper. The paper should be divided into eight sections. Place the paper in the landscape/horizontal format. Using a craft knife, cut the center horizontal fold between the first and last vertical fold. Fold the paper in half.

2. On the back of the decorative papers, run a strip of double-sided tape along the top and bottom edges. Remove one strip of tape backing from each sheet of paper. Center and adhere the papers in each half of the folded maroon paper. Keep the project paper folded. Using a compass, draw a 1³/₄" (4.4 cm) circle in each of the two center panels, 1¹/₄" (3.2 cm) from the paper's top edge. Using a craft knife, cut out four circles.

3. Run a strip of double-sided tape along one edge of the four translucent papers. Remove the tape backing. Slide the papers between the decorative and maroon paper, covering the four circular areas. Adhere the squares into place. Remove the tape backing from the strip that runs along the bottom back edge of the decorative paper. Adhere the papers together.

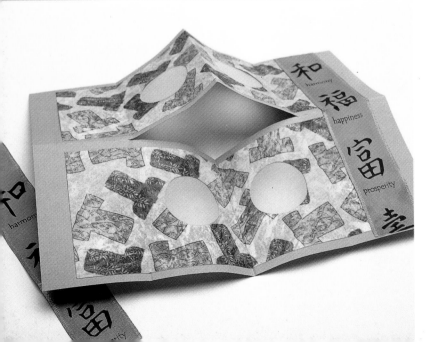

4. Cut the ribbon into two equal lengths. Run each length down the middle of the end panels. Adhere the ribbon ends to the paper with double-sided tape. Turn the maroon paper over with the wrong side up. Cover the end panels with double-sided tape. Fold the paper in half, securing the end panels together.

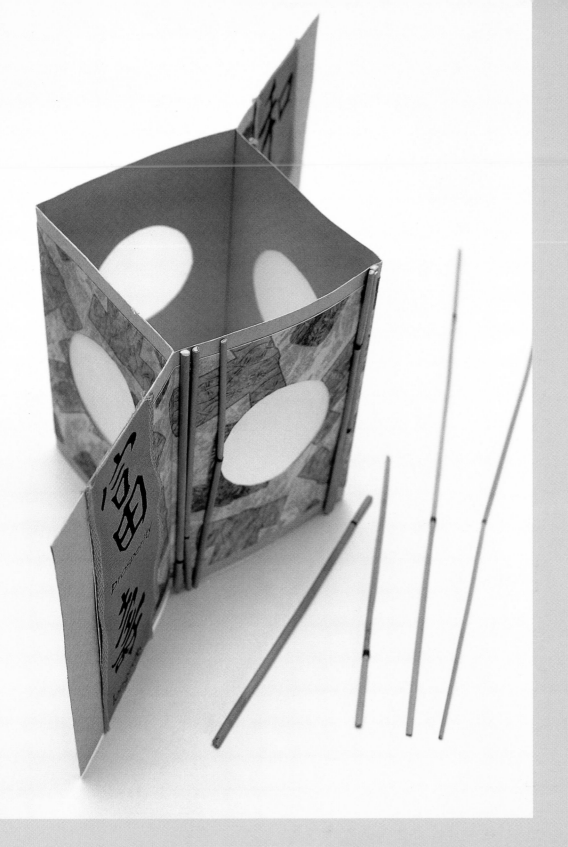

5. Flatten the lantern. Using a craft knife cut the marsh reeds into 4¹/₂" (11.4 cm) lengths. Glue the reeds to the circle panels. When the glue is dry, push the lantern's side panels toward each other and crease the middle folds to form the lantern.

"We've Moved" Birdhouse

Oh, the migratory life of birds! When spring comes around, our feathered friends return. They begin their search for a protective place to build a new nest. Next, they begin the arduous task of raising their young. At summer's end, they are off for warmer parts of the country with a promise to return next year.

If your future plans consist of a moving adventure, why not make a card collection to send to your favorite friends and relatives. Use removable labels so the recipients can adhere your new address right into their address books.

INSTRUCTIONS

1. Place the black paper in the landscape format. Using a bone folder, score a line 2$\frac{1}{4}$" (5.7 cm) from the left edge. Score another vertical line 4$\frac{1}{2}$" (11.4 cm) from the previously scored line. Fold the edges to the center with the short flap on top. Lightly draw a pencil line along the flap's edge onto the flap underneath.

2. Cut a variety of shapes to create a birdhouse approximately 5$\frac{1}{2}$" (14 cm) high and 2$\frac{1}{2}$" (6.4 cm) wide. Use a glue stick to adhere all the pieces together. Place the birdhouse on a sheet of double-sided tape. Using a craft knife, cut along the outline of the birdhouse, trimming away the excess tape.

3. Center the birdhouse along the pencil line and 1" (2.5 cm) from the top of the black paper. Mark with a pencil the top and bottom of the bird-house. Remove the tape's backing from the back of the birdhouse and re-deposit the house on the black paper.

4. Cut a strip of colored paper approximately $\frac{5}{8}$" (1.6 cm) wide. Run a strip of tape on the back.

MATERIALS

- 9" x 11" (23 cm x 27.9 cm) black card stock
- assortment of bright colored paper
- printed address labels
- 6" x 6" (15.2 cm x 15.2 cm) sheet of double-sided tape
- roll of $\frac{1}{4}$" (6 mm)-wide double-sided tape
- flying bird templates (page 101)
- heart template (page 101)
- paper punch
- glue stick
- bone folder
- craft knife
- ruler
- pencil

Remove the tape's backing. Place the paper strip at the bottom and center of the birdhouse. Trim away excess paper from the bottom edge of the black paper.

5. Open the black paper with the birdhouse facing up. Using a craft knife, trim along the pencil line and the left side of the bird-house. Photocopy and cut out the heart template from colored paper. Adhere the heart to the

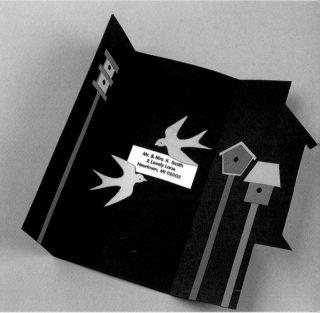

front of the birdhouse with double-sided tape. Turn the paper over.

6. Create three small birdhouses from the bright colored paper. Use the glue stick to adhere all the shapes together. Adhere double-sided tape to the backs. Punch holes for the house openings. Remove the tape's backing and place the houses at varying heights on the side panels. Cut strips of colored paper $1/4$" (6 mm) wide. Adhere strips of double-sided tape to the backs, beneath the houses and to the bottom of the paper. Trim away any excess paper.

7. Copy the bird templates. Color them with markers. Adhere double-sided tape to the backs of the templates. Using a craft knife, cut out the birds. Place the address label in the center of the card. Place the birds with their wings slightly overlapping the label. Mark the bird's position with a pencil.

8. Remove the label. Remove the tape's backing from the birds and re-deposit the birds on the black paper. Using a craft knife, cut along the bird where they overlap the label. Insert the label into the cuts.

*L*ittle Sprout Birth Announcement

Plant markers are used to identify newly planted seeds. They're used to record planting dates and specific names of plants. Here the plant marker becomes a birth announcement, recording the baby's name, date of birth, and weight. These make great bookmarks for grandparents.

INSTRUCTIONS

1. Using a bone folder, score two lines 2¼" (5.7 cm) from the long sides of the yellow card stock. Fold the panels to the center. Unfold the paper.

2. Stamp a number of medium and small daisies in the upper two-thirds of the center panel.

3. Draw a pencil line 2" (5 cm) from the bottom of the yellow card stock and another line 2¼" (5.7 cm) from the previously drawn line.

4. To make the orange flowerpot, use a craft knife to cut two angled lines. Begin the lines on the first drawn line, 2" (5 cm) apart. Angle the lines outward and upward stopping at the second drawn line. Take the 2¼" x 5½" (5.7 cm x 14 cm) orange paper and slip the ends through the two paper slits.

5. To make the flowerpot rim, use a craft knife to cut two ½" (1.3 cm)-long lines ⅜" (1 cm) away from the orange pot. Slip the ends of the ½" x 5½" (1.3 cm x 14 cm) orange paper through the paper slits.

6. On the 4" x 4" (10.2 cm x 10.2 cm) yellow card stock, stamp a large daisy. Cut out the flower. Adhere double-sided tape to the back of the photograph. Remove the tape's backing and adhere the photograph to the center of the daisy. Adhere the daisy to the marker using double-sided tape.

MATERIALS

- 8½" x 10" (21.6 cm x 25.4 cm) yellow card stock
- 4" x 4" (10.2 cm x 10.2 cm) yellow card stock
- 2¼" x 5½" (5.7 cm x 14 cm) orange paper
- ½" x 5½" (1.3 cm x 14 cm) orange paper
- 1⅜" (3.5 cm) circle photograph
- 8" (20.3 cm) planting marker
- small, medium, and large daisy rubber stamps
- yellow, red, and blue ink pads
- small daisy sticker
- 2" x 2" (5 cm x 5 cm) sheet of double-sided tape
- bone folder
- craft knife
- ruler
- permanent marker, ultra-fine

HELPFUL HINT

Use a computer to save time writing out the announcements. Adhere a sheet of double-sided tape to the back of the paper. Cut the paper into strips. The computer paper can then be adhered to the plant markers. Trim the excess paper with a craft knife.

7. Write the baby's birth information on the plant marker using an ultra-fine permanent marker.

8. Using a craft knife, cut a 1" (2.5 cm)-long line along the bottom of the pot.

9. Insert the plant marker into the flowerpot. Then push it through the paper slit at the bottom of the pot to the back of the yellow card stock.

Artist Gallery

The following group of artist friends exchange cards as a sort of visual poetry, often creating and giving them at holiday time or simply sending them off with "Just been thinking of you" or "Have you heard the news?" Ideas, thoughts, and feelings are exchanged, while, love and devotion are expressed toward one another. With a handmade card, we honor the recipient, and, in return, the sender is rewarded in knowing that the card will be cherished. Artists know that the time spent in hand-making something is a reason for loving it more. Stored in a special box, stuck between the wall and doorframe, or pinned to a bulletin board, they are messengers gently calling us back to the people we love.

$\mathcal{M}$other's Day
Luncheon Invitation

Terry Peterson

Fold two sheets of different colored papers in half. Trim ½" (1.3 cm) from all sides of the inside paper. Open the paper and, on the fold, cut a large circle leaving it attached at the 3 and 9 o'clock positions. Decorate the circle to create a flower design. Adhere both papers together. Reverse the circle's fold to create the pop-out. Add a flower stem, two leaves, lettering, and other embellishments to the inside of the card.

Party Invites in the Round

Nancy Marculewicz

Step out from the square and make these charming circular invites. For card covers, Nancy cuts different sized circles from her handmade gelatin nature prints. Attach the covers together by gluing a small area to the left side or by punching a hole and inserting a small eyelet. Decorate the hinged area with brightly colored paper ribbon and dried leaves. For lettering pizzazz, glue letter confetti along the invite's circumference.

Autumn Greeting Notes

Mary Byrom

Ah, the warm, golden colors of autumn are richly represented in these gorgeous leaf notes framed with gold leafed lines. Begin by painting with a wide brush, the front of folded artist paper (100% cotton) with a matte medium mixed with yellow ochre acrylic paint. Let dry. Follow the manufacturer's instructions for gold leafing to make the gold frame. Place newly collected autumn leaves between waxed paper and dry with a hot iron. Paint both sides of the leaves with orange acrylic colors. When the leaves are dry, glue them on the card.

$\mathcal{B}$udding Friendship Note Paper

Barbara Frake

Using simple materials and scissors, charm your friends with this handmade paper stationery. Make the flower petals by cutting heart shapes on the paper fold, varying the length and width of each heart. Construct the flower head by inserting the largest heart shape with progressively smaller hearts. The flower stamens are cut into very long, narrow heart shapes then inserted into the flower. Glue the flowers to the far left side of a sheet of handmade paper. Use paper ribbon or raffia for the stems.

$\mathscr{A}$ long the Garden Fence

Susan Keller

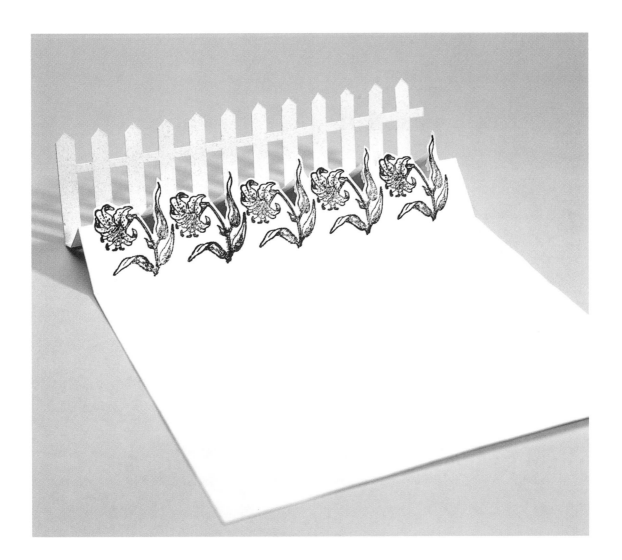

Do you wish for the old days of leaning over a fence and chatting leisurely with a neighbor? Here's an old-fashioned idea in a contemporary letter writing form. Cut a picket fence design along the top of your stationery. Score two parallel lines ¹/₂" (1.3 cm) apart just below the fence bottom. Fold and crease along each line. Unfold. Stamp a line of flowers about 1" (2.5 cm) below the fence. Using a craft knife, cut along the flowers' contour leaving the space between the flower and the paper edge untouched. Score a line along the bottom of the flowers design. Fold the flowers design so they stand upright along the fence pickets.

Templates

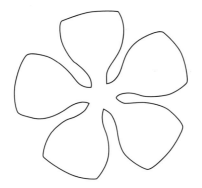

Dried Flower Medallions, page 22

Flower Template

Garden Recipe Cards, page 24

Mason Jar Template

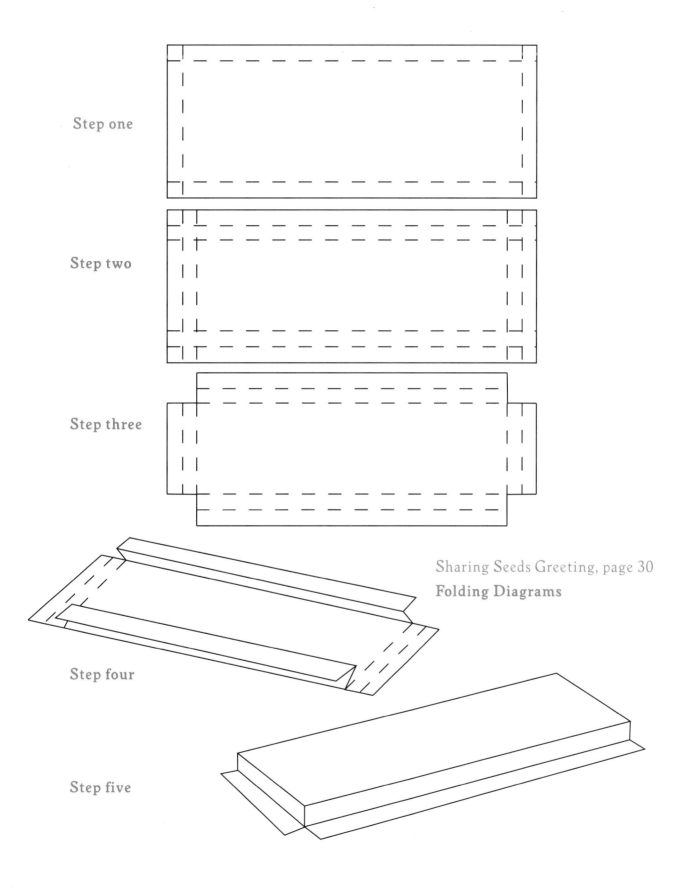

Step one

Step two

Step three

Sharing Seeds Greeting, page 30
Folding Diagrams

Step four

Step five

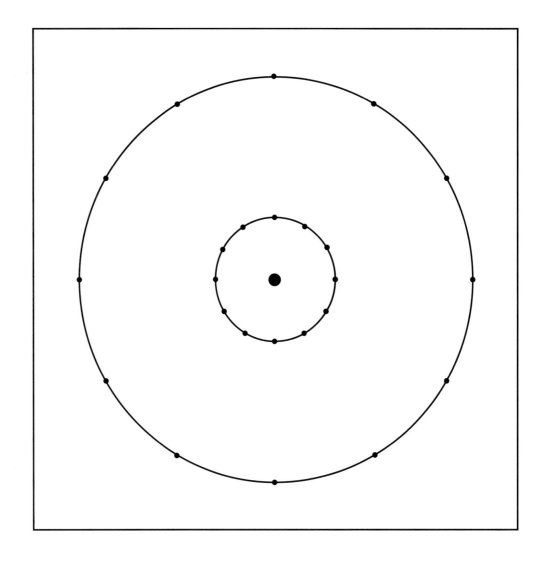

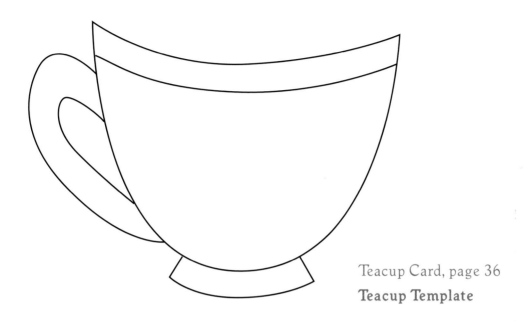

Teacup Card, page 36

Teacup Template

Oval Template

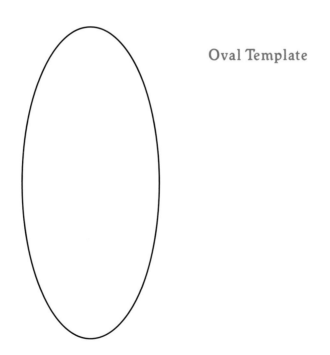

Bee Template

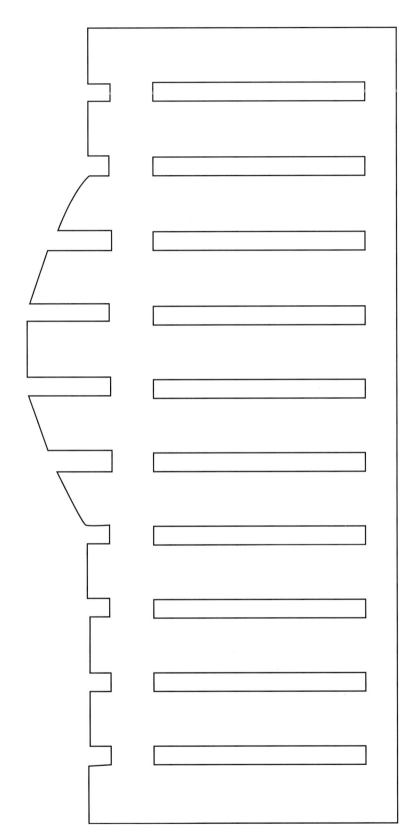

Garden Gate Greeting, page 46

Garden Gate Template

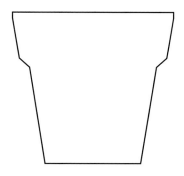

Pop-up Potted Posies, page 56
Flower Pot Template

Bouquet Fanfare, page 58
Flower Panel Template

Posy Packets, page 66
Posy Template

Ladybug Invite, page 74
Leaf Template

"We've Moved" Birdhouse, page 82
Flying Bird Template
Heart Template

Resources

Create an Impression
56 E. Lancaster Avenue
Ardmore, PA 19003
610-645-6500
handmade papers, stamps, art and craft supplies

Daniel Smith
4150 First Avenue South
Seattle, WA 98124
800-426-7923
www.danielsmith.com
exotic and decorative papers, embossed papers, bark paper, 100% cotton rag blank cards and envelopes

Fascinating Folds
P.O. Box 10070, Glendale, AZ 85318
800-968-2418
www.fascinating-folds.com
supplies for paper arts

Inkadinkado
61 Holton Street, Woburn, MA 01801
800-888-4652
www.inkadinkado.com
rubber stamps and stamp supplies

Kate's Paperie
561 Broadway, New York, NY 10012
888-941-9169
www.katiespaperie.com
handmade papers and stationery

Legion Paper Corp
11 Madison Avenue, New York, NY 10010
800-278-4478
traditional handmade papers, fine art paper, digital art paper

Loose Ends
P.O. Box 20310, Salem, OR 97307
503-390-7457
www.looseends.com
papers, packaging, natural paraphernalia

The Paper Crane
280 Cabot Street, Beverly, MA 01915
978-927-3131
imported papers

Paper Source
232 West Chicago Avenue
Chicago, IL 60610
312-337-0798
(stores also in Evanston, Kansas City, Philadelphia, and Cambridge)
handmade papers and stamps

Rock Paper Scissors
78 Main Street, Wiscasset, ME 04578
207-882-9930
fine art papers and stationery

Rugg Road
105 Charles Street, Boston, MA 02114
617-742-0002
handmade papers and stationery

Specialty Tapes

4221 Courtney Road
Franksville, WI 53126
262-835-0748

double-sided tapes, aka D/C Tissue

The Stamp Lady

136 Andover Street, Danvers, MA 01923
978-750-6655
www.stamplady.com

rubber stamps and accessories, fine papers

Twinrocker

P.O. Box 413, Brookston, IN 47923
800-757-8946
http://dcwi.com/~twinrock/welcome.html

handmade papers and stationery

International Resources

UK

T N Lawrence & Son Ltd.

208 Portland Road, Hove BN3 5QT
United Kingdom
Phone: 0845 644 3232
artbox@lawrence.co.uk
www.lawrence.co.uk

Creative Crafts

11 The Square, Winchester,
Hampshire SO23 9ES
United Kingdom
Phone: 01962 856266
www.creativecrafts.co.uk

HobbyCraft

(stores throughout the UK)
Head Office
Bournemouth
United Kingdom
Phone: 1202 596 100

John Lewis

(stores throughout the UK)
Flagship Store
Oxford Street, London W1A 1EX
United Kingdom
Phone: 207 629 7711
www.johnlewis.co.uk

AUSTRALIA

**Eckersley's Arts, Crafts,
and Imagination**

(store locations in New South Wales,
Queensland, South Australia, and
Victoria)
Phone for catalog: 1-300-657-766
www.eckersleys.com.au

NEW ZEALAND

**Littlejohns Art &
Graphic Supplies Ltd**

170 Victoria Street
Wellington, New Zealand
Phone: 04 385 2099
Fax: 04 385 2090

Artist Contributors

Mary Byrom has been gold leafing wood, stone, glass, paper, pottery, paintings and anything else she can get her hands on. She is an artist with an academic and professional background in fine art, textiles, and apparel design. Her work has won awards in environmental sculpture and packaging design. She lives in Southern Maine where she works happily in a simple, sturdy studio built in 1929. She has been concentrating on using metal and gold leaf in her work for the past seven years. She is presently focused on incorporating gold leaf into her landscapes and portraits.

Mary Byrom
102 Wells Street
North Berwick, ME 03906
mbyrom@maine.rr.com

Barbara Frake is a graduate of Boston University's College of Fine Arts where she received her Bachelor of Fine Arts. She is a skilled draftsperson, a graphic designer, and an accomplished artist. Through the years, she has produced a diverse portfolio, which includes architectural renderings, book illustrations, as well as equine artwork shown most recently at Kentucky Horse Park with the American Academy of Equine Art. She is passionate about dogs and horses, carriage driving, and rural life. In her country studio, Frake is inspired to make these subjects the main focus of her painting and drawing.

Barbara Frake
Currierville Road
P.O. Box 273
Newton, NH 03858
barbarafg@aol.com
www.frakefineart.com

Susan Keller graduated high school from the North Carolina School of the Arts. She earned her Bachelor's degree in printmaking from the Maryland Institute College of Art in 1979.

Due to a serendipitous roommate situation, she embarked on a career of medical illustration, which began with rather poorly drawn heart chambers and ended seventeen years later with detailed illustrations of orthopedic surgery.

She is currently having a lot of fun drawing anything she desires.

Susan Keller
8 Summit Place
Newburyport, MA 01950

Nancy Marculewicz has been drawing and painting for as long as she can remember. She is a graduate of Bradford Junior College and received her Bachelor of Fine Arts from Rhode Island School of Design. Along with making art full time, Marculewicz runs workshops on the creative process and gelatin plate print-making. Her work has been shown nationally and can be found in many private and corporate collections. *Making Monotypes*, a recently published book, describes her creative process of making prints from gelatin plates.

Nancy Marculewicz
P.O. Box 177
Essex, MA 01929
jellyroller@earthlink.net

Terry Peterson graduated from the Maryland Institute College of Art in Baltimore, Maryland, with a degree in printmaking. Determined to make a living in art, she has worked as a graphic designer for over twenty years. She now freelances for a variety of local environmental groups. She lives in Annapolis, Maryland, with her husband, Bob, two semi-adult children, Lauren and Eric, and her cat, Pascal. She prefers to dress only in black and white matching her cat and late springer spaniel. Her deep shade garden is a great pleasure in her life and a well-spring of inspiration for her photography and oil painting.

Terry Peterson
523A Epping Forest Road
Annapolis, MD 21401
terry@tcp-design.com

About the Author

Susan Jaworski-Stranc is a printmaker, bookmaker, art teacher, avid gardener, and naturalist. The images she creates reflect her deep connection to the beauty and complexities of nature in all its forms. Educated originally as a printmaker, her extensive portfolio consists of etchings, intaglio prints, linocut prints, and monoprints that portray landscapes and natural textures in both abstract and realistic modes of expression. Her career has evolved over time, and she now applies her printmaking talents to the creation of custom books, journals, and albums. Owners of these books have used them to record their thoughts, hold photos, and house collections of treasured memorabilia. Susan has also created several unique artist books using combinations of innovative designs, materials, and binding techniques. Some of her artist books contain her original writings. Her art can be found in many private collections, and an artist book, titled *SEQUENCE*, was purchased by the Library of the Museum of Fine Arts, Boston and has been displayed at Harvard University. Many of her books can be viewed on her Web site at www.appleciderpress.net. In addition, she has created many craft projects that have been published in books and on craft Web sites. Susan is a member of the American Craft Council and has exhibited in ACC shows on the U.S. east coast as well as numerous other juried craft shows throughout New England.

As a gardener, Susan takes great satisfaction in the beauty of the plants she cultivates. She maintains a special interest in spider chrysanthemums. The feel of the soil, the textures of the leaves, the colors and fragrances of the flowers and vegetables, and the sounds of birds and insects serve as inspiration for much of her artwork.

Susan lives and works in Newbury, Massachusetts. She received her BA in studio art at the University of Maryland, College Park, and received her teaching certificate at the Massachusetts College of Art, Boston. She has exhibited widely in the Washington, D.C., Maryland, Virginia, and New England areas. Susan is a featured artist in another Rockport Publishers book titled *Stamping Tricks for Scrapbooks*, by Betty Auth. Susan may be contacted at 978-465-9896 or stranc@appleciderpress.net.

Acknowledgments

To Ken, my husband, who is my confidant and sherpa in life. To Penelope and Jeremy, my two children who grew too fast and now live independent, successful lives while affording me to have my very own again, sooner than most of my dear friends. To the Creative Spirit for being the good parent that He is, by giving the human race the boot from His Garden so we may plan, create, and work in our own. To Mary Ann Hall, a motivating editor and creative person, whom I met many years ago at the Boston Center for the Arts. To Rockport Publishers for giving me the opportunity to realize my ideas in book form so that I could share with the wider community. Thank you.